MW00934902

How to use this study:

I intentionally kept these writings short so you can use these brief moments to reflect on how certain points impact your daily life.

Use them as a part of your individual daily routine, or maybe read through them as a group. You can read one a day for a few weeks, or take a week on each segment; it is truly at your own pace. Scripture is suggested at the beginning of most segments. Sometimes they have a direct connection to that portion of reading, or they are simply provided as an additional point of reflection. There is always space to go deeper with a passage or a writing, and we hope you will.

Schedule a time to talk through things one-on-one through **jennifermazzola.com** or talk with a group of friends as you journey together.

Before we start:

How do you know when to let go or be done with someone or something?

Do you tend to walk away quickly from relationships when you are hurt, or do you try to fix things and hold tight to others even when they hurt you?

Contents

Introduction

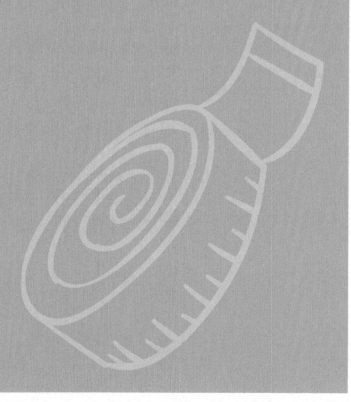

When is Enough, Enough?

A question we have all asked is: When is enough, enough?

When do I need to/when can I let go of someone? When is it okay to give up?

Or maybe it's the other side of the coin: When should a problem be addressed? When is it time to start helping that person?

What we are looking for is a measure. A distance. We want guidance or guidelines on doing life with others. How far should we go?

How do you typically determine when to let go or give up?

I've been in plenty of seasons where I was focused on everyone liking me and being happy with me. There was one particular relationship with a co-worker that seemed like it would never get to a healthy spot. I felt like I had tried everything to dissolve the tension and issues. And it crushed me to not be liked.

But then I read Romans 12:18.

"If it is possible, as far as it depends on you, live at peace with everyone."
(Romans 12:18)

What words grab your attention in this verse?

I was trying the "live at peace with everyone" part, but I missed the qualifier, "as far as it depends on you." I was only supposed to go "as far as it depends on" me. No further. But also, no shorter.

If it is possible, as far as it depends on you, live at peace with everyone.

As I thought back, I could see how in some scenarios I had done all that I could, and I truly had to let go. I felt this verse gave me permission. But at the same time, I could picture friendships where I had given up. I had stopped trying or avoided them out of fear of confronting an issue. I had not gone as far as I could.

Think of your own relationships—your friendships, your work relationships, your parents, your in-laws—have you gone as far as it depends on you?

Sometimes we don't go as far as we could; there are situations and seasons where we can go a little further. We can be the one to apologize. We can be the one to have that difficult conversation. Maybe we've written people off, distanced ourselves or not been really honest, but we know when we are still and listen, we need to take another step toward that person. We haven't gone as far as it depends on us.

Other times, we go too far. We need to stop giving that friend money. We need to stop taking responsibility for responsibilities that are not ours. When we go too far, we don't give others space to mature and learn. Maybe we have become an enabler. We have gone further than depended on us.

Each situation will be different.

For me, it's often ironic. My first guess of how far I should go is rarely the one I walk away with once I've prayed about it. Ultimately, no one can tell you the measure of how far you need to go or when you need to stop going so far. That's between you and God. However, as we dive in, scripture, logic and reason might reveal some insights to help us measure.

Over the next several pages, we are going to look at going "as far as it depends on" me through several relationship dynamics.

- Work
- Friendships
- Church
- Family
- Parenting
- Marriage
- Yourself
- And ... with God

As we explore these relationships, we will ask ourselves tough but honest questions. And together we will look at what changes we may need to make to ensure we are going as far as it depends on us—and only that far.

Reflection

1. What relationships or dynamics are already coming to mind when we talk about when you can let go?

2. Are there particular areas of your life where this principle might be more difficult to apply than others?

3. Growing up, what were you taught about handling problems between you and someone else? How far were you taught to go? Were you raised to have a "screw them" mindset or were you encouraged to be more of a people pleaser?

Zoom In

Before we jump into different areas of our lives where going as far as it depends on you might be applied, let's zoom in on this verse:

"If it is possible ..."

"If it is possible" means it won't always be possible. Some people do not want peace. They do not want friendship. And in some cases, very rigid boundaries need to be drawn. But even in those cases, what IS always possible is YOU doing what YOU can. You can only make sure your side of the street is clean. You can only work with the monkeys in your circus. You can only go as far as it depends on YOU, and their "as far as it depends on" them does not belong to you.

"As far as ..."

Matthew records Jesus having said, *"Whoever slaps you on your right cheek, turn the other to him also. If anyone wants to sue you and take your shirt, let him have your coat also. Whoever forces you to go one mile, go with him two."* (Matthew 5:39-41)

We are often taught that these verses suggest that we should tolerate injustice—a sort of spiritual way of being a doormat. Many see these verses in a very different way like in the way that Martin Luther King Jr., Ghandi, Wangari Maathai and many other non-violent protestors referenced these passages.

There is a "forcing of the other hand" that takes place. As you go as far as you can, there will be an illumination of how far or not far others have gone. If peace is going to be broken, let it be broken by them. You alone, simply

"If it is possible" means it won't always be possible.

being in tune with God's next steps for you, will shine a light on others' choices which will often reveal their struggles for what they truly are. It's actually a very powerful move.

"Your non-co-operation with your opponent is violent when you give a blow for a blow and is ineffective in the long run. Your non-co-operation is non-violent when you give your opponent all in the place of just what he needs. You have disarmed him once for all by your apparent cooperation, which in effect is complete non-co-operation." Gandhi (What Jesus Means to Me, op.cit., 39)

What Jesus is teaching in Matthew is not to be a biblically-licensed doormat. In fact, it couldn't be further from that. He is teaching us to go as far as we can, resulting in a revealing of injustice.

Reflection

1. Can you think of a scenario when you were trying to "live at peace" with someone and they simply did not want to have healing in your relationship?

2. When we think of leaders like Ghandi and Dr. King, we can see how this simple philosophy impacted entire countries. And while many of us will not face a direct conflict with a government or police force, we have all most likely been in a work environment, family situation or friendship where people seemed to prefer an "eye for an eye" mentality. Where people tended to punish others for what they felt was an injustice in their life.

   How have you experienced others' punishments when they have been hurt? How have you passively or directly punished someone rather than applying Jesus' words?

At Peace

"Live at peace ..."

As we begin to look at how this principle plays out in different facets of our lives, it is important to keep in mind that the peace we are striving for is something that might only be felt on our side of the street. We aren't responsible for others' peace.

It is entirely possible to be at peace within yourself while others choose to live in chaos.

Don't confuse peace with being liked by everyone.

Don't confuse peace with being liked by everyone. In fact, that is often the opposite of peace. Peace is an ability to walk through both chaotic and calm seasons with a centered confidence. It's the calm in the midst of the storm; the being carried in His hands. Contentment can be present even while you are not content with circumstances. If we carry around this false idea that people's attitudes and actions toward us can directly impact our personal peace, the very thing we are striving for will elude us.

Reflection

1. What kind of concept do you have of the word "peace?" What does a peaceful life, a life full of peace, look like to you?

2. Have you ever known or do you know anyone that always seemed to be at peace?

With Everyone

"With everyone ..."

This is the tough part. I think we are supposed to apply the principle of going as far as it depends on you with everyone. I've looked at the Greek here—and Paul means everyone. Any human. Now I realize on the outset we assume we do this with everyone, but let's be honest: We aren't that far off from the "expert in the law" who asked Jesus, "Who is my neighbor?"

Stay with me.

In Luke 10, an expert in the law asks Jesus, "How do I inherit eternal life?" This expert should have already known that answer. And he did. The expert responds, "Love the Lord your God with all your heart and with all your soul and with all your strength and with all your mind;" and "Love your neighbor as yourself."

So, Jesus, in agreement says, "Go and do that then" (my paraphrase).

But wanting to justify himself, the expert asks, "But who is my neighbor?"

To which Jesus jumps into the parable of the Good Samaritan, a story about an unexpected caregiver/neighbor.

The point of the story? Everyone is our neighbor.

If we are honest, there are people who are difficult to love. There are some who make the thought of going even one step further sound exhausting, awkward or just painful. And even though we know we can go as far as it depends on us, we just don't want to go that far with certain personalities.

But Paul echoes Jesus here, making sure we don't misinterpret. He doesn't say:

As far as it depends on you, live at peace with those who align with your political beliefs.

As far as it depends on you, live at peace with those of your same ethnic background.

As far as it depends on you, live at peace with those who attend your church, denomination and religion.

As far as it depends on you, live at peace with only those who make you feel good about yourself, praising you and never criticizing.

It's "with everyone." And believe me, I realize this is not always easy. But that also may be part of the point. God uses people with difficult personalities along with uncomfortable circumstances to shape us and develop our own character. I like to call these people in my life "sandpaper people." They are placed in our lives for sanding down the rough edges.

Reflection

1. Are there certain personalities or groups that are harder for you to walk with than others?

2. Do you have "sandpaper people" in your life? Have you ever paused to realize you are probably "sandpaper" for someone else?

Space for Sorting and Sifting

As we go through the various areas of our lives, looking at how we can go a little further in some or maybe have gone too far in others, I hope and would imagine that relationships and scenarios will come to mind. And there might be conversations you need to have. However, I want to stress something: God needs to be your first and greatest filter.

One of the reasons I am so passionate about Jesus is after studying his ministry style you see a theme. He takes life one step at a time. He's always in tune with the Father, managing every engagement uniquely. He might be harsh with one person but gentle with another. There are times he jumps directly to criticism or he simply raises a question or shares a story rather than responds directly. The point is: He approaches each scenario differently, and I happen to believe he does this by staying in tune with where God would guide him. Even when he is being chased and followed by crowds, he consistently tries to get a moment with God.

"Yet the news about him spread all the more, so that crowds of people came to hear him and to be healed of their sicknesses. But Jesus often withdrew to lonely places and prayed." (Luke 5)

In John 10, Jesus talks about a shepherd and his sheep. He says, "My sheep recognize my voice and they follow me."

As you sort and sift through relationships and situations, make sure the first voice you are recognizing is God's. If you aren't in the habit of being still, praying, journaling or some form of getting out of your own head and into a space for God to speak, please consider making that a habit in your life. It takes conversation to learn to recognize a voice. Consistent conversation.

God needs to be your first and greatest filter.

A friend of mine ended up in a very difficult season in her marriage. Her husband left her abruptly. Assuming he would come home after a few days, she decided not to tell her family or friends. She didn't want anyone to think poorly of him when he did come back. But weeks passed, and he didn't come home. She still didn't share his leaving with anyone, not until months later. I was in shock as she shared her story, but what she said has stuck with me.

"As I sat alone, crying until I had nothing left, I realized that this was the first time in my life that I solely relied on God to carry me through something. I went to God first for the first time. It was normal for me to pick up a phone or run to a friend, and there's nothing wrong with that, but I realized that in an attempt to spare my husband future humiliation, the result ended up being that I drew closer to God than I ever had."

I typically run to everyone else first. How about you? It's not that mentors, friends and family can't help or shouldn't help in those seasons, but her experience challenges me to make sure I'm checking in with the main source of wisdom and love first.

As we talk through what it looks like to go as far as it depends on you, make sure you are creating space for that consistent check-in. As you start to measure the distances of your relationships, make sure you're not relying solely on your yard stick.

Reflection

1. When a conflict emerges in your life, who or what is your go-to in terms of conversation, to vent or ease tension?

2. Do you have a habit of checking in with God? If so, how did you develop that habit?

To recap:

- You can only go as far as it depends on you, but that might be further than you think.

- Living at peace with everyone does not mean everyone will like you. "Everyone" means everyone. Yes, everyone.

- God needs to be your first and greatest filter.

Part One:

As Far As It Depends on You at Work

91,250

Read Ephesians 5:8–21

There are two reasons I wanted to start this conversation about going as far as it depends on you in the workplace.

First, my work life was where I struggled most to apply this concept and where my conversations with God about Romans 12:18 initially began. It was work drama that sparked this whole thing. In fact, work drama has been a fairly consistent theme in my life—partly because I'm the common denominator but also because the office tends to be that odd space where we are obligated to deal with others who aren't family. It's a sector of our daily lives that we need in order to pay our bills, unlike friendships or church life.

Second, the number 91,250.

Based on an average lifespan of 72 years, you will spend an average of 91,250 hours working. That's roughly 22.4 percent of our life, not including overtime.

228,000 hours will be spent sleeping, which means you only get an average of 394,000 hours of life awake.

In comparison, we spend …

• 32,100 hours eating
• 4,320 hours exercising and taking care of ourselves
• 3,600 hours laughing
• 42,300 hours of quality time with friends and loved ones

We will spend nearly twice as much time at work than with our spouse, our kids, our loved ones or friends.

Whatever you clock-in to, wherever you arrive Monday morning, that's where you are giving a quarter of your life.

That's a lot of time. And while we might not spend all those hours with our coworkers, employees or the consumers of whatever we offer the world, we will spend some quantity with them. And learning what as far as it depends on me needs to look like at work can make all the difference in the quality of those hours.

Reflection

1. When you think of your workday, are there certain relationships that cause more tension than others?

2. Have you experienced a work dynamic that made you struggle to come to work every day?

3. What has workplace conflict looked like for you?

Know Who You're Sitting With

Read Psalm 139

I believe work is a part of God's plan. It's meant to be more than a paycheck. It's a space to utilize our unique God-given design. But that also means we get 91,250 hours to interact with other people who are as equally uniquely designed.

When I took a course in Human Growth and Development, we spent time exploring science's search for the self. What makes us, well, us? Are we just a pile of DNA? Can you predict who we are or how we will turn out through observing how we are raised?

We were divided into groups and were asked to artistically demonstrate on poster board our concept of "the self." As we worked together, we developed a list of all the factors that contribute to who we are:

• Biology
• Parenting
• Experiences/Trauma
• Culture
• Education
• Economics
• Religion
• Environmental Factors

And each of these factors had subsets. Then, we tried to discuss how much each of these facets plays a role in developing who we are. For example, is our biology 70 percent or 50 percent of who we are? Some would say we are mostly nature and others would argue we are almost entirely nurture. There is no definitive answer. We are all of these things, yet none seem to be defining.

You can always find an exception to the rule. Still, all these factors make us, us. And that means: Just as you are shaped by so many things, so is the person sitting across from you at that conference table.

You may not even be aware of all the factors that shape your responses, your body language, your habits—and, for sure, your coworkers probably aren't considering the myriad of dynamics that shape you when they interact with you. Your boss isn't wondering how your parents disciplined you when you react the way you do to being called into their office. Just like you most likely have no clue what is really going on at home, in a marriage or with someone's kids when they are annoying you through email.

I'm not saying this is an excuse for poor behavior. In fact, I think we need to learn to address situations more often and in a healthy, mature manner that leads to results. I'm simply acknowledging that when you sit across from someone at work, you not only sit across from them, but from the army of experiences and family system factors that make them who they are.

We can be fairly complex.

The Psalmist says, "I am fearfully and wonderfully made; your works are wonderful, I know that full well."

My question is: How many of us know that "full well." If we can't recognize our own temperament, demeanor and attitude that we bring into the workspace, how can we expect others to be keenly aware of how they come across or know how their delivery makes others feel?

The first step to going as far as it depends on you at work is to know yourself as well as you possibly can.

The first step to going as far as it depends on you at work is to know yourself as well as you possibly can.

What is that thing that always bothers you?

Have you wondered why that one work problem seems to follow you even when you change jobs?

You've noticed how "so and so" always does "such and such," but have you taken the time to observe your "such and such?" Because I would bet that you are a "so and so" to someone else.

The work of learning yourself can be difficult, but you would be surprised how much peace you can find at work when you are able to clearly see yourself.

Example: I'm an only child. I grew up in a fairly calm and quiet household. However, we didn't always say what we were thinking or feeling which has made conflict tricky for me. Contrast that with two of my coworkers from my previous job. They both came from large blended families and, for the most part, they shared openly and sometimes harshly when opinions varied.

During a meeting, these two coworkers had a disagreement and you could feel the tension in the room. I couldn't get out of there fast enough. So, I was completely confused when a little while later they were laughing and heading out to lunch together.

As an only child, if I didn't get along with you, I went home. And at home my imaginary friends thought I was awesome, and I never had conflict with them because they did what I said.

I asked my coworkers, "Did you guys not feel that in that meeting?"

"Feel what?" one of them asked.

"The tension!?" I said.

"I mean, we disagreed but it's over now," said the other.

A. Maze. Ing.

It may sound so silly to some, but for me, it was mind-blowing. All of the sudden I could recall countless work scenarios where I avoided conflict or could not get out of a meeting fast enough.

As I learned more about my personality, and why I react the way I do, so many other things made sense. "That's why that always makes me angry!" "That's why I've struggled with people who say those types of things." "That's why I've always gotten that response during a review." The good and the bad. It makes more sense as I seek to know how I am made full well.

"So and so" is "so and so" for a reason. And so are you.

As I learned more about my personality, and why I react the way I do, so many other things made sense.

Reflection

1. Are you generally quick or slow to react in work situations?

2. How often do you take time to consider the things that impact how others might respond?

3. When was the last time you took a personality profile test or read something about personalities, different types of intelligences or some other resource examining why we do the things we do? What was your response?

That's Just So and So

Read Colossians 3

Speaking of "so and so," another way to go as far as it depends on you at work is to make sure you are avoiding the "so and so trap."

Well, that's just Bob. He will never change.

Well, that's just Suzy. She can't help it.

While yes, there are things about our management style or our personality that are VERY difficult to change. This phrase is akin to the church world's phrase of "bless their heart." And I know for me, I often use it as a license to avoid confrontation or honesty. It's more of a "giving up" phrase than a "letting go" phrase. And there's a difference.

This really hit me when I realized certain people within my work community felt this way about me.

"Well, that's just Jenn. She's always gonna be critical and negative."

They weren't wrong, but I didn't want them to see me that way. While I am for sure a glass-half-empty personality, as long as they interpreted what I meant to be constructive as destructive, our organization and team would not be vibrant.

The most difficult thing about raising my teenage sons is that they are in a season of life where they think I know nothing. I am old and outdated and have zero clue what I'm talking about or how to navigate life. They only want to see life through their lens. They already know so much. And when it comes to work dynamics, I often behave like a teenager. I can receive criticism with a teenage internal eye roll. I can choose to ignore advice during a review because "they have no clue," or I can grow up, listen and avoid being "so and so."

Example: One day my boss called me into his office.

"I want to share with you something that was said about you. Apparently, you ignored Mrs. Jane Doe in the hallway. She said hello to you, and you didn't look at her but just kept walking."

"I was walking to the bathroom. I had to pee."

He loved me enough to say, "I get it. I know your heart, but you tend to have a serious expression on your face when you are walking with something else on your mind or headed to get something done. This isn't the first time someone has mentioned your effect. I'm just saying that when you are in the hall, even though it's just their perception, make an effort to keep your head up, smile and be engaging."

I was so annoyed. Was he asking me to be fake?! This was ridiculous. But he was right. My pride didn't want him to be right, but he was. I've always discussed with my kids and others that perception is a portion of our reality, so how was this any different?

I worked on it. The irony? Later, a new boss said to me, "I want to make sure you're out front and connecting with people. You bring such great energy and joy."

I can't even.

Don't give up on people.

Don't give up on people. Even a negative, intensely-walking-to-the-bathroom-person like me can modify a few things.

Reflection

1. Do you have a "that's just so and so" in your office?

2. Have you ever caught a glimpse of how you were truly coming across? Has anyone ever taken the time to honestly share how others see you?

3. Have you ever tried talking with "so and so?"

Use Your Voice

Read Colossians 3 *(again)*

"Have you ever tried talking to them?"

We generally get that question when someone is being a buzzkill to our complaining or gossiping. And, for me, the answer is generally no with a litany of reasons it wouldn't matter.

One key part of going as far as it depends on you is releasing your ownership of others' responses.

If you have an issue with someone—ask yourself, "Have I prayed about this?" then, "Have I owned my stuff?", and then, "Have I tried talking with them?"

We should have a rule: Don't complain if you haven't used your voice.

Don't like a politician? Vote.

Don't like a policy at work? Have an adult conversation with a supervisor.

Frustrated that person drops the ball all the time? Talk to them.

I say that, and I'm still a chicken. I have said before that I am all talk. I get all fired up and have all my opinions about what someone should or shouldn't do, but when there is a chance to use my voice with the correct person, I am a chicken. And not just a quiet chicken but a smile-and-pretend-nothing-is-wrong chicken. Then, I go right back to being irritated and opinionated.

Most people don't speak up because they think it won't matter. And we aren't always wrong. But that's the problem. The verse isn't "go as far as it depends on you unless the person is stubborn" or "go as far as it depends on you unless you are guaranteed to see the change you want." That's not the passage.

If we know we need to say something, we need to develop the maturity and courage to be honest.

"Do all things without murmurings and disputing." (Philippians 2:14)

I can murmur with the best of them.

"Let no corrupt communication proceed out of your mouth, but that which is good to the use of edifying, that it may minister grace unto the hearers." (Ephesians 4:29)

That word "corrupt" can also be translated as rotten or useless. The word "edifying" is drawn from a word that references "architecture" and "structure."

What are you building with your words?

When I think of how many useless murmuring conversations I have had, I realize how many missed opportunities I had to actually build something.

Yes, we need to pray about conversations, think through our thoughts and seek wise council, but then, we need to go as far as it depends on us and use our voice. It at least guides our feet in the right direction, even if they choose to go a different way.

Reflection

1. Do you typically complain about work or coworkers?

2. How are you when it comes to speaking up and addressing situations?

3. Why do you think we shy away from using our voice at work?

Stay in Your Lane

Read Proverbs 4

"Let your eyes look straight ahead; fix your gaze directly before you. Give careful thought to the paths for your feet and be steadfast in all your ways. Do not turn to the right or the left; keep your foot from evil." (Proverbs 4:25)

One aspect of work and, honestly life in general, where we go too far can be our observation and assessment of others. We can "know your lane" all day long, but when our head turns to the left or right to evaluate, envy or judge how others are running their race, we might be going too far.

How do you handle the success of a coworker? How do you handle the success of a coworker you struggle with? Ever felt like some team members get away with way too much?

When we find ourselves consumed with what others are doing, not doing or how they are being handled, we can fall into what some therapists call "compare and despair," or, bad math.

The equation of my life and my work choices cannot be balanced by becoming fixated on what others are doing. When someone is praised or recognized for an accomplishment, it is very easy for us to start practicing bad math: "Well if she gets X-Y-Z, then that must equal X-Y-Z for me."

When someone adds something to their life, we often apply that to our lives by subtracting from our own value. Or maybe we project bad math on to them: "If he was recognized for A-B-C, then it can only be because he compromised E-F-G."

We can passively punish someone or compromise the character and integrity of our own work.

I have a tendency to drift, to look at the left and right, rather than fixing my gaze directly before me. The danger of forcing our way into another's lane is that it causes us to stumble. It's super natural (not to be confused with supernatural) for me to notice what others do and don't do.

A coworker of mine once told me, "I know you have a ticker. A tally sheet where you keep score of things that I do that bother you."

"I don't need a sheet. It's always in my head," I confessed.

It's not something I'm proud of. God constantly has to fix my gaze; taking my head in his hands and directing my attention back to the only things I can manage—my attitude and my actions.

We are going too far when we find ourselves keeping a literal or mental score card. We are going too far when we are judging others, formulating bad math. We allow their choices to add or take away from our race. There is extreme value in paying attention to what you are paying attention to, so make sure you know where your gaze is fixed.

Reflection

1. Have you ever caught yourself paying more attention to your "left or right" than paying attention to your own work?

2. Have you done some bad math in the workplace?

3. Have you been a victim of someone else's bad math?

To recap:

- You spend 91,250 hours at work. It's important you are aware of how you spend that 22.4 percent of your life.

- You are fearfully and wonderfully made, but do you know that full well? We are uniquely knit together, but so is the person who sits across that conference table from you. Realizing you don't fully know others and knowing yourself well will create a space for grace to grow in your office.

- Don't fall into the "that's just so and so" trap.

- Don't complain if you haven't used your voice.

- Don't look to the "left or right." Fix your gaze on your lane.

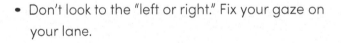

Part Two:

As Far As It Depends on You with Friends and Family

Cliques and FOMO

Read Proverbs 13:20, 17:17, 18:24

Growing up, especially through my teen years, friendships and school dynamics created the majority of the drama in my life. I remember thinking, "When I'm an adult, friendships will be much easier." Well, they aren't. In fact, sometimes I think they are more difficult to find, more awkward to maneuver and can be more painful than any locker room or high school hallway scene.

Maybe it's the only child part of me, but finding healthy, deep friendships gets harder every year. I have a tendency to push away and avoid friendships that are worth fighting for, and I fight too hard for friendships that have run their course.

One way we go too far in friendships is not managing our expectations, so when a friendship ends, or we realize we aren't included somehow, we take it way more personally than we should.

Jesus had different levels of friendship. I realize this sounds odd, and like Jesus had his own clique, but he did. So, it's funny how when we notice on social media a group hanging out, or a smaller group that seems to always get together, we hop on the bad math train and take a ride.

When flipping through the gospel accounts, we find that Jesus was followed by hundreds of people, trained 70-plus (Luke 10), worked closely with 12 (Mark 3) and seemed to have an exclusive relationship with only three (Matthew 17). This ironically mirrors what social scientists in the 1990s would cite after their studies on how many social connections we could cognitively maintain.

The most famous of these studies was done by anthropologist Robin Dunbar. His theory became known as Dunbar's Number. He theorized that we could hold around 150 casual relationships—this would be like our social network.

Within that group, we would on average have about 50 in our close active network, out of which 15 would be considered our sympathy group. From there, five would be considered our core group or support clique.

A couple hundred followers = 150 casual relationships

70 disciples = 50 close network

12 apostles = 15 sympathy group

3 exclusive friendships = 5 core support clique

My first job in ministry was as a youth pastor.

My predecessor asked me, "What will be the first thing you work to do with this group of youth?"

I didn't hesitate: "I'm gonna break up all these cliques." I said that with 21-year-old sass because the word "clique" immediately drags me back to teen years when I didn't feel on "the inside" at all.

His response: "I hope not. Small groups of close intimate friendships, or cliques, are so important to teenagers. They shape their identity and give them a sense of belonging and safety. It's when they are rude to others not within their clique that it's an issue. I would hope you wouldn't actively try and split up healthy small groups of friends."

Maybe we struggle with friendships because we expect to be in someone's group of three when we would make four. Maybe we see the 12 and are overwhelmed with FOMO (Fear of Missing Out), or maybe we struggle in a different way. Maybe our life experience has taught us to be guarded and let no one in, which creates a void because we are designed to be in community. Maybe you prefer the 150 casual relationships, or the 50 close network isn't completely terrifying, but the 15 or the 5? "No, thank you." It's safer in the rafters of Dunbar's Number.

I think if we are all honest, we do want at least a few folks in our corner. At least one or two BFFs who totally get us, with whom we can completely let our guard down. What I have seen in adult friendship land, though, is a lot of being envious of other friendships or finding ways to defend our own isolation.

We aren't going far enough when we don't allow anyone in, but it's too far to expect to be a part of every clique.

Reflection

1. In general, are friendships difficult for you to establish?

2. Have you ever found yourself being envious of others' friendships?

3. Do you have a strong, healthy clique?

Friendships Do End

Read Ecclesiastes 3

I remember reading that the average friendship lasts five to seven years. I would joke with friends, "You've got maybe three years left within my friendship countdown." I was half-serious, half-joking.

When I realized that friendships had seasons, that you weren't necessarily supposed to be close to everyone for all eternity, it was actually a huge revelation. I had friendships come and go, but it always seemed to be someone's fault. If someone moved and the friendship changed, in my mind it had to be because one of us was a terrible long-distance friend (admittedly this was generally me). If there was tension in a friendship and social circles changed, it wasn't enough to realize that people drift and just change in general. It seemed like one of us had to find a source to blame. It was as if it wasn't possible for two decent people with a decent friendship to change and cause the friendship to shift without meaning to hurt anyone. Unfortunately, except for the rare handful of long-term friendships, that is what happens.

Yes, some friendships end because of betrayal. Sometimes the friend feels abandoned in a time of need, but most likely, the friendship shifted before that even happened. Those moments might have emerged because we don't know what to do when we don't have something to be mad about.

People move. People get married. People have kids. People change jobs. People change churches. People pick up new hobbies. New people come into circles and others get closer. In the midst of all this shifting and changing, friendships shift and change too. That's okay. The goal should be to do our part to communicate honestly, and celebrate change with one another, rather than punish each other.

We don't know what to do when we don't have something to be mad about.

Have you ever had a friendship where you don't see or talk to each other for months, but when you get the chance to reconnect, it's amazing? Like you never skipped a beat? Most likely, it's because you wrapped up those friendship seasons well, honoring the changes life brought. On the other side, have you ever been in the grocery store and literally changed aisles to avoid someone? Maybe even left the store? Why? It's because something is off in the friendship, but it's not being talked about or acknowledged. So, we limp along in this awkward friendship for sometimes years, wasting time and energy.

It's okay for a friendship to change, or to be over altogether, as long as you've gone as far as it depends on you to communicate and be vulnerable and honest. When we hold too tight, we may be going too far and denying God the space to bring new people into our lives, or we may be allowing a friendship that already ended to keep taking up mental real estate for no real reason.

Reflection

1. What do you think about the idea that friendships last an average of five to seven years? Have you found this to be true in your own life?

2. Why are some friendships harder to let go of?

3. Can you think of healthy ways to release a friendship that has finished its season in your life?

It's Time to Grow Up

Read 1 Corinthians 13

What is your typical response when you have been hurt within a friendship? How do you manage feelings of betrayal when you realize someone has talked behind your back, or when you feel left out?

I was sitting at Starbucks with a friend. We had recently been in a disagreement. This was a rarity in my life. It was rare because I typically just ran away from friendship conflict, but it wasn't until this coffee date that someone gave a name to my pattern.

"I was ready to be blacklisted."

"Huh? What do you mean?"

"Well, that's what you do, Jenn. I've seen you do it for years to a lot of people. You disagree. Someone doesn't react how you want or do what you want, so you blacklist them. They aren't allowed to exist anymore."

While I would like to think I have grown up since this observation was so kindly pointed out, the truth is, my gut reaction is still to turn my back, build up a wall and act like I can't see you.

We all have methods of self-defense. Some of them obvious and overt while others are super passive and may be such a part of our routine that we don't even realize we use them.

Over the years, I have shunned some very amazing people. People who loved me. However, in my immaturity, I couldn't let go of whatever it was that bothered me, so it was just easier to shut them out.

The word "punish" sounds extreme, but it is what we do. We remove our approval. We make passive comments or sideways jabs. If we were going to help them with something, we make ourselves unavailable. Perhaps we chime in just a little more when others are talking negatively about that person. We frame, we maneuver and we angle. My strategy is to blacklist people who hurt me, but you might have another technique.

1 Corinthians 13 is probably most well-known for the "love passage"—that litany of attributes that Paul uses to describe love. However, there is a part after all the love stuff that challenges me every time I read it.

"When I was a child, I talked like a child, I thought like a child, I reasoned like a child. When I became a man, I put the ways of childhood behind me."
(1 Corinthians 13:11)

Essentially Paul is saying, "Hey, you distracted group of Corinthians, here is what real love looks like, so it's time to grow up and start doing it."

I will say, as years have rolled on, there have been a couple of scenarios where I wanted so badly to just have that person disappear from my life, but I pushed through. I didn't stop at the blacklist measure. I went a little further, and it paid off. Those friendships are so much deeper and richer. Not only in spite of conflict, but because we worked through it.

Reflection

1. What is your go-to technique for handling conflict with friends or family?

2. Have you punished someone for hurting you? Can you recall a time you were the one being punished?

3. Are there areas in your friendships and family relationships where you just need to grow up?

Remaining an I in the Midst of a We

Read Psalm 133

For many reasons, these principles can get a bit trickier when dealing with family dynamics. Family can be much more difficult to navigate when it comes to figuring how far or not far to go.

Family Systems Theory is a facet of psychology that emphasizes family relationships as an important factor in psychological health. The idea is that our family tree reveals so much more than genealogy, and that healthy change for families and individuals is best addressed within the context of the whole system.

While studying Family Systems Theory in graduate school, I remember learning the terms "enmeshment" and "differentiation" as they related to helping families. My professor explained, "Enmeshment is when things are so complexly tangled, when boundaries and borders within the system are not present, that you cannot separate the 'I/me' part of your life with the 'we/us'. Our family rules and scripts define us, and we overidentify with the values of the system. Our role is to guide clients closer to differentiation. Does anyone know what that is?"

Someone responded with what I was also thinking: "A separation from the system. Solid boundaries and borders, clearly seeing how the parts of the system are separate."

"No," she responded. "You would think that, essentially taking the opposite of how we view enmeshment, but the differentiation in family systems is more like helping people be a sponge. Helping them see how the family system does shape them (soaking up the water) but also giving them the ability to release what is no longer needed in their life (wringing out the water). It's not separating from the family but learning to be an 'I' in the middle of a 'we.' "

Healthy families stay connected while also maintaining their own boundaries and identities.

We can easily gravitate to an "all or nothing" approach with family, but healthy families stay connected while also maintaining their own boundaries and identities.

There are times of abuse or neglect that require us to draw very clear and solid boundaries with family members, and friendships for that matter. I am not suggesting we "remain in the midst of a we" when there is danger.

Still, there is value in taking an honest evaluation of how we are moving within our family system because we can only control how we move.

Families develop these cultures, almost a rhythm or dance, if you will. We get so used to this dance that we can be unaware we are even doing it. Your family may have patterns of arguments, family mantras or rhythmic ways in which they have dealt with certain things that can extend back generations.

"The next generation would know them (God's teachings), even the children yet to be born, and they in turn would tell their children." (Psalm 78)

Over and over again, we see this idea in the Bible. The idea of passing things along to future generations. Even more, one generation's actions affect future generations. Each family has a dance, and some of our families have been doing the same dance for a very long time.

Part of going as far as it depends on you with your family is getting to know and recognize your system better. What is your family's dance? What is your part in that dance?

If you decide you are going to step closer to health and depart from norms established in your family system, both you and your family will have to learn a

new dance. The system is set up to do an auto-reset.

You take a step closer; they will most likely take a step back.

You take a step back; they will probably take a step closer.

Our family systems develop set-points for relating to one another, so when you disrupt those set-points, you are disrupting the system.

I was part of an amazing weight loss group. We all really struggled in our relationship with food. As we went on this journey together, we noticed how difficult it was to go to family gatherings. Even our family meals had a dance of their own. A friend of mine in the group asked if, for his birthday, they could skip the cake and ice cream.

"What in the world do you mean? Who are you trying to become? Our family is big. We are just big people. What are you trying to do?" a family member responded.

My friend said, "What if we are big people because we all choose to eat poorly, treating food more like an experience than fuel? I've never seen a person eat carrots and celery who is still big and say, 'Well, I guess we are just big people.' "

Food may not be a dance for your family, but trust me, your family has a rhythm. Because of this, if you try to introduce new moves, you might get pushback. Just remind yourself that the system is resetting, and it may take a while. You are simply going as far as it depends on you.

Reflection

1. Do you think family relationships can be more difficult than friendships?
   If so, why?

2. Share a little about your family system and how you see yourself fitting into "the dance" of your family.

3. Have you tried to bring change to your family and met resistance?
   What was that like?

Honor Thy Father and Mother

Read Exodus 20:1-17

How are things with your parents? What is that relationship like for you?

I think as adult children we still really want to see our parents love us and also thrive in their own lives. We want to see that they are still learning, growing and getting the most life has to offer. Deep down, we want good things for our parents.

I can remember making a list/prayer for my mom. She was struggling with a few things, so I was praying for her. It looked something like this:

Father, I pray for freedom for my mom. Freedom from ...

I proceeded to list off about five things that I had deemed she needed to be "set free" from. God broke right into my heart and said, "Rip it up. You do not get to dictate a list for your mother's life. You don't get to mandate your version of freedom."

So, I tore off the bottom portion of my listed items and left it as: "Father, I pray for freedom."

Do we realize that they are their own people with their own story, and we are just a blip on their journey's radar? This also means they have their own fears, insecurities and struggles. We can have so much grace for a struggling friend. We would never give up on our struggling children. However, we can carry so much frustration and anger toward those other humans that are normal strugglers-who-also-happen-to-be-called-our-parents.

Just as they might still be seeing you as that rebellious teen, are you seeing them beyond their role as your parent?

I was leading a women's small group several years ago, and we were reading a book about really digging into what made you—as a woman and accepting and stepping into the way God made you. There were chapters on body image, work, friendships, daddy issues and our mothers. The author actually used two chapters when she arrived at this topic. The first of these two chapters mapped out the importance, but also the difficulty, of the mother/daughter relationship. After leading dozens of groups of women, I can say that from my experience, most women struggle with their relationship with their mother. Nearly 80 percent every time, every group. So as we approached these chapters, I knew it was going to stir up something in our group. After we got through the initial chapter, we moved on to the second part in her segment on moms and daughters. It was a chapter of prayers. Prayer after prayer of forgiveness for our mothers. We each had our own experience with those chapters, but mine has stuck with me.

I sat down to read and pray through that chapter, but as I read, I realized these weren't flaws I needed to forgive my mother for; I suddenly saw them as hardships that she had to endure with her own mother. God gave me a glimpse into how she was raised and what she experienced.

One of the Ten Commandments reads, *"Honor your father and your mother, so that you may live long in the land the LORD your God is giving you."* *(Exodus 20)*

You often hear sermons citing, "This is the only commandment with a promise." Have we ever wondered why?

The Hebrew word for "honor" in this passage is defined as "to be heavy, weighty or burdensome." For me, I'm reminded that honoring my parents

won't always be easy, or might at times feel heavy, weighty or burdensome. Whether I like to admit it or not, I will most likely feel burdensome to my children at some point. I share this passage to remind people that when they feel that frustration, they are not alone. In some ways, it's supposed to be that way.

We go too far when we forget that our parents, or people for that matter, have an entirely separate story and journey with God, and that we are simply a fraction within that journey. We go too far when we demand, ignoring dignity and volition, that people make the choices we want for their life. We don't go far enough when we ignore the command to honor our parents.

Reflection

1. If you had to choose one word to describe your relationship with your parents (now or in the past), what word would you choose?

2. Have you ever caught yourself trying to dictate how God should move in the life of someone else?

3. What role does forgiveness play in the dynamic between you and your parents?

4. What does "honor" look like in your family relationships?

To recap:

- We aren't going far enough when we aren't willing to allow anyone in, but it's too far to expect to be a part of every group.

- Friendships can change, or be over altogether, as long as you've gone as far as it depends on you to communicate and be vulnerable and honest.

- Don't punish.

- Your family has a rhythm. If you try to introduce new moves, you might receive pushback. Just remind yourself: The system is resetting, and it may take a while.

- We go too far when we forget that our parents have an entirely separate journey with God and that we are simply a fraction within that journey. We don't go far enough when we ignore the command to honor our parents.

Part Three:

As Far As It Depends on You at Home

Prelude

When the boys were little, and they would see Sal and I hug one another, they would run under our legs and yell, "HOUSE!" I honestly have no clue why that was the word they chose, but it's fitting that one of my prayers is that the boys feel like they were raised in a safe and loving home. I can't control how they interpret their upbringing, and we have money set aside for their therapy later in life, but I can take an honest evaluation of how I show up at home. I can go as far as it depends on me.

I have heard it said, and I agree, that "The greatest gift you can give your children is an example of a healthy marriage." No marriage and no home are perfect. We each will carry a little baggage from the way we experienced life during our developmental years.

A DISCLAIMER: Not everyone is married. Not everyone has or will have children. Our culture seems to mandate these facets of life's journey, but I believe you can have a richly abundant life without ever becoming a spouse or parent. I also believe you can get married and not have "a marriage" just as you can have a child but still be so far from "being a parent." These next segments simply explore a few dynamics we might encounter if we do choose to be married or have children. But the lessons contained within these types of relationships apply across our lives so don't skip them.

Apologies Don't Have Buts

Read James 5:16, Matthew 5:21-26

How good are you at apologizing?

Our marriage stalled out several times early on. We hit some vortexes of circular arguments—the kind that keep coming up and never seem to resolve. We fell into some fairly numb seasons when we were essentially roommates instead of spouses. While there were many factors and lots of immaturity that contributed to this, we stumbled upon a very simple principle that has made a difference.

Apologies don't have "buts."

Sal used to be the worst at apologies. By the way, he approved me throwing him under the bus. It would sound something like this:

"I'm sorry you are so sensitive."

"I'm sorry you don't understand … can't see … don't get … etc."

Take an "I'm sorry" and add an addendum, and you have Sal Mazzola's conflict-resolution method.

Meanwhile I would say:

"I'm sorry, but you … but they … but last week … but last year … but …"

An apology, if sincere, does not need a caveat. If you are sorry, you should simply be sorry.

When we find ourselves rattling off a litany of excuses, we are trying to justify our choice. We diminish our partner's hurt or frustration. We minimize the damage we have done.

When you start to examine "as far as it depends on you," let your apologies come up short. Just say "I'm sorry."

Reflection

1. Have you found yourself stuck in a cyclical argument pattern—the same argument over and over?

2. Be brave. Ask your spouse or someone close to you, "How do I typically apologize?"

3. Do you owe anyone a very simple apology?

Energy Levels

Read Proverbs 19:11, 1 Thessalonians 5:15

We are living beings. All living beings survive off energy. Everything requires energy. To grow, we need energy. To walk, we need energy. To think, we need energy. To be married, we need energy.

We all have finite energy. As we lose energy throughout the day, we need to consume things that give us more energy, but that energy will run out too.

This is the reality for us, animals and plants. It's the human ability to think, to move beyond basic instincts and to engage beyond our basic brain levels that set us apart. We get to choose. We get to choose how to expend our energy and how to refuel. We also get to choose how to respond to others' levels of energy.

For many of us, when we get home, we don't have very much energy left. When we are walking through a stressful season of life, we might have even less energy than on a typical day. That energy shortage can sometimes have us functioning at a less than ideal level. So, when I'm going as far as it depends on me, my energy is a factor. The same applies to everyone in my home, in my office and in my world.

Here's how this plays out: If Sal and I both come home at 90 percent, we are probably going to be fine.

But let's say I have one of those days, and I'm running at 40 percent. This causes me to be short-fused. I snap at the kids; everything Sal says gets on my nerves; and I say some snarky comments. Now, Sal gets to choose. Does he stay at 90 percent, or does he look at me and think, "Ah, okay. I see. I'm not gonna take this. I'm dropping down to match your 40 percent?"

When we are both operating at our best, we just go skipping along. However, when one of us—regardless of how aware we are—decides to bring a lower level response to our space, the other drops right down too. No matter if it was out of frustration or hurt. Why? Because it's exhausting trying to maintain a 90 percent day by yourself. The reality is, though, if even just one of us can decide we are going to go as far as it depends on us to keep things level, then we might get a little closer to lifting one another up. Imagine what would happen in a marriage where both people were committed to doing their own individual best to recognize the level in the room and going as far as they can to encourage and support.

Sometimes it's as simple as giving someone a heads up that you are tired or feeling off for whatever reason. A while back, I started sending Sal warning texts to let him know about my day. It might be that I'm having one of those days or that the boys and I aren't communicating well, or that I'm just in a funk. It's not about the why or an expectation to fix it, it's just about letting him know, "Hey, I'm coming in at about 10 percent today, so I might seem extra grumpy."

Years later, we were talking with a couple about some frustrations they were experiencing, and Sal said, "Ya know, a while back Jenn started sending me these warning texts from time to time, and they really helped me. I was able to think through how I could be more helpful when I got home, or how I could maybe deal with the kids so she could walk away for a little bit."

You can't control the level at which they set their attitude, but you can control how far you go to commit to raising the bar every time. I had a friend once say, "But it's exhausting taking the high road every time." Yes, it certainly can be. But it is a road worth traveling in the end.

Sometimes it's as simple as giving someone a heads up that you are tired or feeling off for whatever reason.

Reflection

1. In your own home, have you noticed how people respond when you have a bad day? Have you noticed how you typically respond when others bring their frustrations home? Are you brave enough to ask?

2. What was the last scenario when a warning text might have been helpful? Do you find yourself expecting people in your home to be able to read your mind or interpret your moods?

Change Takes Time

Read Galatians 6:1-10

How long do you think it takes someone to change?

A moment? A few days? At least a week?

The reality is we can make some choices that last a lifetime and others that we sustain for just a few months. Sometimes we have one great habit for many, many years, and all the sudden we switch over to a randomly poor pattern of behavior.

When I work with couples, I have what I call a "six-month rule." They want to know how long they have to wait to see results or how long they have to try before something can look different or someone can be trusted. I always respond with "six months." I have zero scientific reason for this. Although, I'm sure I could find some article somewhere that would get close to my measure of time. My general thought is this:

Anyone can change and work on any issue for a month or two. Some people can sustain changed behavior for three months, but when you see a real difference for a full six months, you most likely are witnessing actual change. Granted, that person who had an affair can go right back to that behavior a year or more later. When I see someone who wants to know how long it takes someone to change, I ask them to give it six months.

I also ask for six months of effort.

To me, it's important that you are able to look at yourself in the mirror—only you and God staring at the reality of your situation—and ask yourself, "Have I done everything I can do? Have I gone as far as it depends on me?"

If you have kids, will you be able to look at them and say, "I did everything I could to have a healthy marriage."?

We want to read one book, have two counseling sessions, take three aspirin and call it "changed." That's also why we tend to end up back where we started before we've given it six months. We do not give things time.

As we read about Biblical figures that went from this to that, from sorrow to praise, from in prison to ruling nations, from running in fear to leading thousands, it's sometimes hard to understand how much time it really took for those things to happen because the story may be short.

Joseph was in prison for three years.

Moses was in Midian for 40 years, then another 40 with Israel wandering the desert.

Some scholars guess that David hid in a cave for almost a decade.

When I start a new workout routine, all the sudden I'm a cyclist or a spin person or a runner or whatever I'm into at the moment. The reality is, though, I've gone to three classes. The same thought applies to hobbies and diets. I'm excellent at short-term change. Six months is longer than it sounds.

If change is hard for me to sustain, it's also going to be hard for those I love. It's going to take time to trust that change, too. We can't assume two weeks means all is well, but we can't give up without more effort than a month.

When I suggest a six-month plan to work toward life change, it's often met with wide-eyed sighs. And I get it; it sounds like forever. Sometimes scenarios are so unhealthy, it is not safe to give conflict more effort or time. Being able to look back and know we have done everything we can, not just for one month or three months, but long enough to allow space for real work and change, is a precious gift to ourselves and our families. When you measure how long you can wait and work on this or how far it depends on you, start with true effort and measure out six months.

Reflection

1. What are you wanting to work on in your marriage or life? Can you make a commitment to follow through on at least one small step for six months?

2. How much time and space do you give people to change? Are you a "one and done" kind of person, or do you give up too quickly on the change you can contribute?

3. Why do you think most couples find themselves in repeat patterns?

It's Not Personal; It's Parenting

Read Ephesians 4:25-26, James 1:19-27

I never realized I had anger issues until I had children. Clarification, I never realized I had anger issues until I had children that could talk back to me.

I was the typical "my kids will never tell me 'no' or disrespect me" person. You know those people. You might be one. Somehow this dream of mine never came to pass. My kids push my buttons in every way possible. I didn't realize I could yell like I can yell or lose my temper the way I can lose my temper. My voice changes when I talk, and I become an entirely different person. I become like a possessed pea soup spitting person. (Pop Culture Reference)

But the reality is: It's not personal; it's parenting.

Why does every ungrateful complaint make me fume? Why does every smart-mouth comment drive me crazy? Why does every missed opportunity, lack of effort or reminder of sheer laziness drive me up a wall? Because somehow, I have made these things personal. As if my teens are doing these things to me.

I want the boys to be smart, articulate, hard workers, determined, courageous—the list goes on. But I forget that those things have to be forged. They are trying to figure out who they are and where they fit in all while their hormones and bodies are all over the place. They are doing exactly what I did—pushing against my parents for the sake of learning how to push and talking back while I tried to find my own voice. Trust me, I have called and apologized to my mother many times.

It doesn't mean I shouldn't address disrespect; that's part of guiding them. It doesn't mean they don't need boundaries or consequences; that's part of training. Still, it doesn't mean I need to take everything personally.

When they were little, I caught myself parenting from embarrassment. I worried they weren't reaching benchmarks and how people viewed their behavior. My parenting wasn't about them. It was about how others saw me.

Now, I'm parenting from disappointment. Every time they don't see their potential, value or worth, it breaks my heart. I get disappointed in them and in myself. Again, making parenting about my expectations and journey, not theirs.

So many times, I need to take a deep breath. Step back. Realize they are not doing this to me and parent a little less personally.

I can remember when the boys were around three and four. I was in graduate school and working. I ended up with a free day and decided to make the most of it. I planned a day at the zoo. I could picture the whole day in my mind, and it was going to be perfect. Off we went. I don't have to tell you that the day went nothing like I had planned. This devastated me. I didn't get enough time with the boys as it was, so for the day to be ruined broke my heart. As I recalled the story to the counselor I was seeing at the time, he said, "So they were acting like normal four-year-olds?" Yes. They were. But it wasn't how I wanted the day to go! Could they not see that I was making up for lost time? Building memories? That I had planned the perfect day? No. They couldn't. And they still can't.

They are being teenagers. They are not doing this at me or to me. They are just trying to figure out life.

Have we forgotten the years when we knew everything?

"Do not take to heart all the things that people (teenagers) say, lest you hear your servant (or teenager) cursing you. Your heart knows that many times you yourself have cursed others." (Ecclesiastes 7:21-22)

It's not about letting our kids get away with dysfunctional behavior. It's about parenting from a position where I remain the mature one rather than reverting to acting like a child myself. When I'm seeking to go as far as it depends on me as a parent, I need to remain the adult. It's about standing outside the storm while loving and guiding them, but not letting them pull me under too. When I do find myself feeling and responding as if they are doing this to me, I have to remind myself that it's not personal; it's parenting.

Reflection

1. Do your kids push your buttons? What is your typical response when it comes to frustrating moments with your children?

2. Some personalities take things more personally than others. What type of personality are you? Do you feel like your kids (or for that matter, anyone in your life) are doing things to you? Do you generally take things too personally?

3. If you find yourself responding to your kids in an unhealthy way, what are some ways you can call a timeout to collect yourself and make sure you are remaining the adult in the room?

Consequences and Follow-Through

Read Genesis 2:15-17, Galatians 6:7-9

"I caught her lying so I told her she couldn't go to the sleepover."

My friend called me after her preteen daughter had been caught in a lie. The rules had been laid out prior: "You are not allowed to such-and-such, or you will not be able to go to Jenny's sleepover Friday." Her daughter did such-and-such, so, she told her she wasn't allowed to go to Jenny's.

How simple is that?

Your kid leaves a folder for school at home; he gets a zero.

You say you are leaving the house at 8:30 a.m., but your teenager isn't ready; she gets left at home.

Your young adult child runs out of money; he has to become financially responsible.

It sounds so easy. You present the concept clearly, map out the consequences and simply follow through.

Here is what would have gone through my head if my daughter broke the rules and shouldn't go to Jenny's:

"Jenny's mom has all that food for the kids. She is expecting my daughter. Am I really going to bail on Jenny's mom? Plus, my daughter seems sorry. I think she really gets it this time. Maybe I can just take away screen time for 30 minutes."

Please tell me you are rolling your eyes. Because I am. I stink at follow-through, and both my kids and I have paid the price.

We have to let consequences do their work. It's how we learn. When I soften, shelter or remove consequences from my child's choices, I am going further than it depends on me. I get why we do it. No one wants their kid to get a bad grade. We all make mistakes. Even more, follow-through is exhausting. Sure, we say no video games, but they nag and whine until we cave. What about when the consequences mean we have to sacrifice our plans, or when the consequences reflect on us? We don't want to look like "those parents."

"For the moment all discipline seems painful rather than pleasant, but later it yields the peaceful fruit of righteousness to those who have been trained by it."
(Hebrews 12:11)

From the very beginning of time, God set up a system that requires consequences for us to truly learn and thrive. Even in the lavish nature of God's grace, especially His grace through the cross, He still allows our choices to have consequences.

It's so difficult to watch our children bear the burden of their choices. When my mom would punish me, she would add, "This is way harder on me than it is on you." Something I completely see now.

We all miss the mark, but when we don't allow the gravity of consequences to do its work, we can easily deceive ourselves and make it too comfortable for others, ended up staying stuck together in dysfunction. When I stretch into as far as it depends on me for my children, I'm overreaching. I'm rationalizing their misses. I'm going too far and robbing them of their own as far as it depends on them lesson.

We have
to let
consequences
do their
work.

Reflection

1. Did you ever get away with something growing up, and when looking back, you wish you had actually learned your lesson?

2. Where do you struggle with allowing consequences to bear fruit? Why do you think that is difficult for you?

3. Are there areas in your life, or in the culture of your home, where you are avoiding the reality of missing the mark?

To recap:

- Apologies don't have buts.

- Recognize when you are matching lower levels of communication and reactions and try to raise the standard for that day.

- Change takes time. Don't rush ahead with expectations; allow time to reveal what is really going on.

- It's not personal; it's parenting. Make sure you are responding, not reacting. Remember: You are the adult.

- Whenever possible, allow natural consequences to play out, letting our kids feel the real weight of choices. Be clear and upfront with expectations and then simply (Ha!) follow through. Do what you said you were going to do.

Part Four:

As Far As It Depends on You with You and Him

Just Show Up

Read Genesis 1, Luke 5:16, Matthew 6:33

For the first 10 years of being a Christian, I had a strenuous relationship with the phrase "quiet time." I bought every devotion under the sun. I would journal for two weeks, and then that would fade. I would play worship music until I just didn't anymore. I looked up various reading plans like reading through the Bible in a year, reading through the Psalms, reading the words of Jesus. If I heard someone mention their amazing conversations with God, I would immediately want to know what they did and set myself up to do the same. And I would do most of this stuff for a week, maybe two or sometimes three, but it would always fade. I was spending all my efforts and energy trying to figure out the right way to spend my time with God rather than just focusing on spending the time. And each time I realized, "It's been a while since I've prayed or read the Bible for myself," then guilt would settle in.

When I started to simply show up, things started to change. I say "simply" but I do believe there are some caveats. First, you need to show up your way. And that may look very different through various seasons of your life. You may want to journal or you may hate journaling. You might read over a morning cup of coffee or talk to God through your morning commute. The key is showing up.

Second, you need to show up, somehow, every day. Try not to fixate on how long you are meditating or how much you are reading. In fact, if you can, remove your watch or clock and just be. But be every day.

Show up, somehow, every day.

Third, and this is more a personal preference, form a habit. If you can snag the same time each day, planted in the same place, your body will learn that is your time. You'll notice how precious that time becomes as your physical body actually realizes this is your pattern.

People have often asked me, "How do you know if God is speaking to you? I'm not sure I've ever heard God."

Here's how this works (an analogy):

As I write this, I have been married for almost 20 years. I can recognize my husband's voice in the middle of a crowd, when his allergies are acting up or even in a whisper. Sal's voice is so familiar to me that I don't even realize I'm recognizing it, but my brain automatically lets me know "That's Sal." There are other voices all around me that I couldn't pinpoint, lots of people who could call me while they have a cold, and I would have to ask who it was. Sal's voice is familiar.

God's voice works the same way. The more I am simply around, the more I am in His presence, the more familiar His voice will become, and the faster I can jump into a real conversation. A stranger is strange because I have no context to frame a relationship around. If I find myself frustrated because I'm not hearing from God, I need to ask myself if I'm even showing up. That doesn't mean that spending time each day solves all our problems. No more than talking to Sal every day gives us a perfect marriage. But a couple that intentionally sets aside time to communicate, typically has a much more vibrant marriage than most.

When God speaks, creation responds. Look at what all was accomplished in Genesis 1 through what "God said." But we have to show up to listen. There is not a formula for how to show up. Try a whole variety of ways to connect to God—just be sure to show up. That part depends on you.

Reflection

1. Where are you in developing the habit of setting aside time with God?

2. What hinders you from developing that time?

3. Have you ever compared yourself to others in terms of spirituality?

Let God Be God

Read 1 Peter 2

Jumping back into Romans 12: *"Do not repay anyone evil for evil. Be careful to do what is right in the eyes of everyone. If it is possible, as far as it depends on you, live at peace with everyone. Do not take revenge, my dear friends, but leave room for God's wrath, for it is written: 'It is mine to avenge; I will repay,' says the Lord."*

I had this one situation where a group of women had gotten together and said some not-so-nice things about me. Over time they said more of those things and to more people. One day, someone decided to share with me the things that were being said. This was not your everyday, run-of-the-mill gossip but some very serious lies and accusations. When one particular woman in the group learned that I knew what she had been saying, she came to me. She promised me she would stop saying those things and that she would stop talking about me altogether. She was told that if she continued to be divisive and spread false information, she would not be permitted to serve in her current volunteer capacity. Of course, I was still super mad. That wasn't enough. I wanted some type of payback. I had been wronged.

As usual, I ranted about this one day to God. As I was picking up after an event at the church, I was talking to God about how unfair everything was in this scenario. How could this woman get away with this? Why wasn't more done? How was this okay?

God gently broke in, "I am not saying this is okay. I'm not okay with what was done. Just because someone does something, that doesn't mean I'm okay with it. I give them choices just like I give you."

You would think this revelation would calm me, but nope. The next several mornings my quiet time was anything but internally quiet. I was still angry.

But one morning, I was tired of being angry. I didn't want to cry or play through conversations in my head anymore. I wanted to let it go. I had yet another conversation with God and felt Him respond, "I will handle this. Trust me. Let go." I could physically tell a difference after that morning; the weight was gone. That was around 8 a.m. about a week after the initial blow-up.

At 10:30 a.m., I got a text from a friend. Not just any friend. A friend I had not been close to for a few years; someone I had recently connected with again. This was also a friend that had zero clue what had been taking place at the church. I had not shared anything with her. This was also a friend that happened to work in the exact same office as the woman I had the conflict with.

The text read: "Hey, I'm not sure what's going on, but you may want to talk to so-and-so. I'm sitting here outside our break room, and she is telling our office staff some terrible stuff about you."

(Insert wide-eyed emoji.)

There is a theme throughout the Bible about the dynamic between darkness and light. We read about light shining through. We see a repeated idea that what is in darkness will come to light. Things will come to light. Always.

Notice I'm not saying that "Things will come to light quickly" or "Things will come to light when and how you want them to." I'm more thinking that *"What you have said in the dark will be heard in the daylight, and what you have whispered in the ear in the inner rooms will be proclaimed from the roofs."* (Luke 12)

Part of going as far as it depends on you is learning to trust God with others.

Part of going as far as it depends on you is learning to trust God with others. To let God do God's thing, in all things. We want to run ahead. We get a picture of what should be done or how conflict should be handled, but sometimes we are trying to go too far. Allowing God's plan to unfold always brings what is in darkness to light.

Right after our theme verse, Romans 12:19 says, "Do not take revenge, my dear friends, but leave room for God's wrath, for it is written: 'It is mine to avenge; I will repay,' says the Lord."

We tend to shy away from the word "wrath." In this context, its literal meaning is "proper punishment." And note the words "leave room"—meaning give space, get out of the way, allow an opportunity.

There is no way I could have orchestrated that friend of mine walking by that break room at that exact moment, or to back up further, the fact that we had reconnected after years in the first place. God is not a puppet master playing games with us, but He is a God that keenly rides the rippling waves of others' choices to offer light.

Don't press further into situations where God is asking you to "leave room." God is not saying that He's okay with some of the choices people make that hurt us. He is asking us to trust Him.

Reflection

1. Have you ever had a strong desire for revenge/vengeance?

2. Is there a current situation you are struggling to allow God to bring to light?
   A situation you are trying to manage or control?

3. Can you think of an example when God's method for handling a situation
   revealed itself?

Bring Your Whole Self

Read Romans 8

My sister-in-law experienced her fifth miscarriage. She and my brother-in-law had gone to countless doctors, tried every shot, technique, procedure available. She was exhausted. When they shared with us about yet another loss, she told me, "I can't even talk to God. What would I even say?"

My advice was, "Start there. Tell God you can't talk to Him. That you don't want to talk to Him. That you are angry. And whatever tears or shouts or expletives that follow, bring those too."

I think one of the gifts of not being raised in the church is that my understanding of a relationship with God is way less tainted by countless years of lessons about the right and wrong ways to communicate with God. For many, God is distant and removed. For others, He is some mystical being that seems to only emerge during a heightened state. And for some people, God is an eternal gold star giver, where you only get what you have earned as you check off His ever-demanding list. Any vantage point other than all-encompassing love will most likely have you limiting what you bring to God.

We overcomplicate how far we can go with God. We over analyze what we say, when we say it. We place logistics around our relationship. The creator of the universe can handle our anger. The One that placed the stars in the sky and put the planets in orbit can handle a cuss word here and there. He is not shocked. He is not standing by with a list of requirements of worthiness that must be fulfilled before you speak.

When we read in Romans 8, "For I am sure that neither death nor life, nor angels nor rulers, nor things present nor things to come, nor powers, nor height nor depth, nor anything else in all creation, will be able to separate us from the love of God in Christ Jesus our Lord." Paul is painting a beautiful picture of what going as far as it depends on us looks like for God. Notice Paul doesn't add qualifiers. There are no contingencies or addendums. Your emotions don't separate you. Your pain doesn't keep you at arm's length. Your mistakes, while they will always reap consequences, they are not permanent gap creators. Luke quotes Paul in Acts sharing a similar sentiment, "He is not far from any one of us. For in him we live and move and have our being."

When you watch a movie with friends, what do you talk about after? Do you ever find yourself saying, "Did you see that part where ... ?" or "Did you hear it when she said ... ?" Of course, they did; they were watching the movie with you. But we talk about these things because we just shared something together. God wants to watch the movie of your life with you daily. He is a part of every line, every plot twist, every epic moment and crazy scene.

There are about a million and one reasons we hold back when approaching God. Maybe we've been taught there are certain thoughts you can't say, or only certain people that have access. The irony is: Jesus came to "tear the veil," to remove the divide, and in many ways some church leaders have been trying to hang the curtains back up for centuries.

Maybe we struggle to be vulnerable during our time with God because God hasn't met our expectations. Perhaps we correlate God's presence with getting what we want. Don't confuse God's love with your desired response from Him. But even that's okay to express. As a teenager, I swore I would never tell my children, "Because I said so." I'll give you one guess as to how long it took me to utter those words as a parent myself. My kids don't have to understand or like my methods, and I give them space to share their thoughts, but a disagreement never dilutes my love for them. I think God is okay when we don't agree, and He's a big enough Father to shoulder our angst.

Don't confuse God's love with your desired response from Him.

There is no formula to communicating with God. But it is pointless to try and hide your whole self. Job didn't. Read the Psalms and notice the ups and downs of David's words. You'll see moments of doubt, moments of fear, shouts of praise, declarations of trust. It's all in there. Perhaps that's why Jesus uses children as an example. Through innocence, a child, not yet learning the tricks and masks the world mandates, approaches God as their whole self. Life hasn't taught them not to yet. I don't know a small child who doesn't ask a million questions, tell you what they do or don't like, or cry out when they are hurt or angry. Before the world provides lessons in coping or social norms, children just show up. They don't know not to.

Part of going as far as it depends on me in my relationship with God is making sure I am being real with all my feelings and thoughts, showing up as my whole self.

Reflection

1. What were you taught growing up about how to communicate with God?

2. Are there certain emotions or thoughts you feel you have to hide from God?

3. Have you ever had an argument with God? How did you feel afterwards?

If It Looks Like Duck and Quacks Like a Duck ...

Read Psalm 139

I have always struggled with my weight. My first memory of feeling like I was "fat" was in third grade, and the roller coaster never really stopped. I feel like I have tried every diet and workout trend on the planet. After college and getting married, I really neglected my health. About four years after my youngest son was born, I realized I was more than 100 pounds overweight. I utilized about a million reasons why it was more difficult for me than most to eat right and exercise, and I gave myself about a million more pep talks that seemed to barely have a three-week effect. At one point, someone gave me a book about how we view and understand food, and early in the book the author plainly stated, "Overeating is gluttony, and gluttony is a sin. Not physically taking care of our body is slothful, and slothfulness is a sin."

Now, the reality of why food had become a comfort for me, and the chemical makeup of my body, is way more complex. And the way God views these things is beyond theologically complex, so I'm in no way pronouncing judgment on myself or anyone else—but the simple fact was: The author really simplified my struggles. And it hurt.

How I treat my body is just one of the things I've had to examine through honest evaluation. I've had to take an honest look at my work ethic, my attitude with coworkers, my parenting and my sex life. I've had to stop dressing up sin. I've had to ask God to help me see my issues as they actually are, without my rose-colored glasses and the fog of excuses.

Sin literally means "to miss the mark." There is a cartoon strip where a character is shooting arrows at a fence and his friend approaches.

Noticing his friend keeps missing the bullseye, he points out the fact. In response, the archer simply grabs a can of paint and draws new targets around the already missed arrows. Such a great illustration for how we tend to manage sin. Rather than own and adjust to the reality that we missed the mark, we grab our paint bucket of rationale and pretend we hit the intended target all along.

Part of going as far as it depends on you with your own growth and maturity is to get a clear picture of where you are—and honestly evaluating the gap between where you are and where you want to be. It's not about beating yourself up. God leaves space for grace to accompany you on your journey to your best self, but self-deception only has you taking steps back or at the very least staying stuck. And we are masters at self-deception.

Scientists of all types are constantly studying our behaviors, patterns and choices, trying to uncover why we do what we do and trying to help us break free of the many destructive cycles we find ourselves in. There are countless books that help reveal our subconscious tendencies and endless podcasts and lectures illuminating what we are often times too entrenched to see. I'll leave the psychology of self-evaluation to the experts. My aim is to have you pause long enough to get at least a clearer picture of where you are, both now through a set aside time of self-reflection and in daily small situations as you make it a habit to practice seeing clearly.

What's really going on with you at work?

What's that reaction really about?

PART FOUR | SECTION FOUR | IF IT LOOKS LIKE A DUCK AND QUACKS LIKE A DUCK ...

77   78   79   80   81   82   83   84   85   86   87   88   89   90   91   92   93   94   95

Where are there actually obstacles vs. excuses?

Where are you are trying to rationalize something that simply isn't benefiting you?

What are you holding on to that you should have let go of years ago?

There are countless questions that get us closer to talking with our true self, but there are also countless distractions and avoidance techniques.

I would love to tell you that one book magically turned around all my struggles with weight and health. But it didn't. There had to be many more honest statements run across my heart before I began to really see what was happening. A doctor would reference my knee or back problems, my pregnancies signaled potential future issues, and one day a friend said, "If your kids were running into the street, could you even run to save them? If you fell in a ditch that was just a few inches deeper than your height, could you pull yourself out? Do you see the reality of diabetes and heart disease?" It sounds so brutal, but it was his way of helping me see the real target.

Maybe it's a conversation with a mentor or a trusted friend. Perhaps it's asking a boss or coworker what it's really like to work with you. It starts with a desire to see things as they really are, inviting God to search, test and reveal.
(Psalm 139)

Reflection

1. Can you recall a time when you realized you had been blind to something about yourself? What brought about that realization? What was the result?

2. Have you ever observed someone rationalizing dysfunctional patterns? How did it make you feel? Where have you seen that in yourself?

3. Where are you currently "painting targets" around the reality of where you are missing the mark?

PART FOUR | SECTION FOUR | IF IT LOOKS LIKE A DUCK AND QUACKS LIKE A DUCK ...

77   78   79   80   81   82   83   84   85   86   87   88   89   90   91   92   93   94   95

Full Well

Read Psalm 139 *(again)*

Part of seeing yourself as you truly are is to know yourself full well. Typically, we see a portion of Psalm 139 hanging in a baby nursery or used in a conversation about body image with a group of teenage girls. "I praise you because I am fearfully and wonderfully made," but the verse too often gets cut off there, leaving behind, "Your works are wonderful, I know that full well."

This sparks two questions for me:

Do you know yourself full well? That you are uniquely knit together and made? (from earlier in Psalm 139)

Do you know that you are wonderful? And that part of knowing yourself full well is to know that you are fully loved?

Your personality, your tendencies, your experiences, your auto responses—all of these combine with your biology, your genetics and environmental factors to make a totally unique you. I thought about taking up knitting one time. When I thought on the psalmist's choice of words, "You knit me together," I thought, "Hey, it would be cool to see what all knitting entails." Yep, it entails a lot. Honestly, too much for me. Major applause to all you knitters out there.

It's complicated, and I'm just referencing a basic technique. Knitting a rag or a potholder would be hard enough for me; I can't even imagine a scarf or a sweater. My point is: You are a fairly complex being. It might be good to get to know yourself.

People have all sorts of reactions when I suggest they take personality tests. Some hate the idea of being labeled or put in a box. Others (like myself) have always loved them, making sure to flip straight to the quiz sections when we read teen magazines or never missing a chance for an online quiz. I think there's a balance somewhere. My goal is never to define someone by giving them a number or a color or a cute animal reference. The goal is to explore as many slivers of the traits that make them, them as possible. To get as fully well known as possible.

The more I discover how God has made me and how my experiences have shaped me—the more I am able to see both my gifts and my struggles—the more I can start to spot where I am blessed and cursed. Or if anything, it's a reminder that not everyone thinks like me or sees the world through my lens. Digging into my personality and patterns creates a grace factory for my life. It makes me feel a little less crazy and helps me to remember that others might not be as crazy as I thought either.

The more you learn about yourself, the more you realize how radical God's love is. To realize God made a decision to have the opportunity to walk in relationship with you, knowing you full well. Fully knowing who and how we are, He still calls us wonderful and loved. Not in spite of ourselves, but because we are His work.

Ever had a favorite artist or musician? Ever read about or discovered the meaning behind their song? Ever spent time learning about the medium they chose for that canvas and why? The more we discover about a piece of art, the more clearly we see the reflection of the creator. You are a part of creation, a fingerprint of God's work in the world. The more you discover yourself, the more you seek to know full well, the more you will see how deeply loved you are.

Reflection

1. Have you ever taken a personality quiz or studied your personality profile? What did you discover about yourself?

2. What is your favorite thing about your personality? What is your least favorite thing? Is there a relationship between these two aspects of you?

3. Have you ever noticed a theme in the way people describe you?

To recap:

- Just show up. Create a consistent time and space to meet with God daily.

- Allow space and be patient when it comes to consequences unfolding from others' choices. Let God be God.

- Bring your whole self before God. There is no need to hide or sugarcoat your thoughts, fears, worries or frustrations. God can handle ALL of you.

- Be willing to see sin for what it really is. Be willing to own your struggles while also owning the lavish grace and love poured over your life through Christ.

- Get to know yourself a little better. You are uniquely, fearfully and wonderfully made. There is purpose behind your personality. Be intentional in learning all you can about how you have been knit together.

jennifer mazzola

If it is possible,
as far as it depends on you,
live at peace with everyone.
ROMANS 12:18

jennifermazzola.com

---

jennifer mazzola

When I was a child, I talked like a child,
I thought like a child, I reasoned like
a child. When I became an adult,
I put the ways of childhood behind me.
1 CORINTHIANS 13:11

jennifermazzola.com

---

jennifer mazzola

Contentment can be present
even while you are not content
with circumstances.

jennifermazzola.com

---

jennifer mazzola

If we know we need to say
something, we need to
develop the maturity and
courage to be honest.

jennifermazzola.com

Let's continue the conversation!

I would love to stay connected through other studies, setting up a Spiritual Direction session, or joining you for an event or retreat.

Be sure to check out **jennifermazzola.com** for other books, study series, and services.

Made in the USA
Columbia, SC
30 July 2021

42673624R00059